If I Really Wanted to

Grow Closer to God

I Would . . .

RACINE, WI

If I Really Wanted to Grow Closer to God, I Would . . .
ISBN: 979-8-88898-111-5 - *Paperback*
ISBN: 979-8-88898-112-2 - *Hardcover*
ISBN: 979-8-88898-114-6 - *Ebook*
Copyright © 2023 by Honor Books
Racine, WI

Cover design, interior design, and editing by Faille Schmitz. Manuscript prepared by Hafer & Associates, Colorado Springs, Colorado.

INTRODUCTION

Are you longing to grow closer to your Creator and gain understanding concerning His great love for you and His purpose for your life? If so, then this book was written for you.

The journey to knowing God is a personal one. However, this book has been designed to provide simple tips and insights to help you on your way. Can we guarantee that you will find what you are looking for? Of course not, but God can. The Bible encourages the true seeker to "Come near to God and he will come near to you" (James 4:8). If you are truly searching for Him with an open heart, you will find what you are looking for.

May God bless you as you embark upon and endeavor to renew your spiritual journey.

If I really wanted to
Grow Closer to God,
I would . . .

Be on the Lookout for Miracles

MIRACLES TEND TO HAPPEN TO THOSE WHOSE EYES ARE OPEN TO SEE THEM.

Does God part seas anymore? Or feed people with manna from heaven? Maybe you haven't witnessed a miracle of biblical proportions recently. But then again, maybe you haven't had your eyes open wide enough to see both the spectacular and the simple, but amazing, acts of God right in front of you.

You already know this first-hand, don't you. After all, isn't it a miracle when a person's life—when your life—is changed because of a brand-new response to God's love?

So open your eyes and heart to God's miracles. Expect them, want them, and enjoy them when they occur. *When.* Not *if.* Because as you grow closer to God, your life will be nothing short of miraculous.

The whole crowd of disciples began joyfully to praise God in loud voices for all the miracles they had seen.

LUKE 19:37

If I really wanted to
Grow Closer to God,
I would . . .

Strive for a Personal Relationship with Him

YOUR RELATIONSHIP WITH GOD IS ONE THING YOU SHOULD TAKE PERSONALLY.

There is a big difference between knowing about God and truly knowing Him personally and directly. Take time to be still in God's presence, and ask Him to fill your head and your heart with His love and wisdom. Books, sermons, and music can all help you experience God's presence, but they should only be pathways to God, not destinations unto themselves.

You can't read a movie review, for example, and get the same experience as seeing the movie yourself. And you can't truly understand someplace on the globe by pouring over a travel brochure. You must go to the place and enjoy it firsthand.

That is His call to us—simply to be people who are content to live close to Him and to renew the kind of life in which the closeness is felt and experienced.

THOMAS MERTON

IF I REALLY WANTED TO
GROW CLOSER TO GOD,
I WOULD . . .

ADMIT WHEN I'M WRONG

THERE IS NO PLEA BARGAINING WITH GOD.

No one likes to admit doing wrong. And yet, when we confess our mistakes to God and to those we have hurt or offended, we are, in a sense, admitting that we are not perfect and that we need God's grace in our lives. It is a sad person who insists that he or she has no need of God's grace. Such a person will never know the sweet comfort of collapsing into God's arms and hearing Him say, "I forgive you."

Don't let pride and denial limit your possibilities. God is wise and good. Clear away all that might keep you from knowing Him fully.

If we confess our sins, he is faithful and just and will forgive us our sins and purify us from all unrighteousness.

1 JOHN 1:9

SET MY "PET GRUDGE" FREE

Maybe that "pet grudge" was cute when you first got it. But not anymore. It has grown big and demanding and ugly. Its whining and complaining annoy you and those around you. And it keeps leaving those unsightly stains on your soul. So, it's time to set the grudge free. After all, God says that we must not be resentful (2 Timothy 2:24).

Open your heart's door and shoo the grudge away. Then forgive the person who gave it to you in the first place. You will feel better. Your heart will feel lighter. And if that grudge ever comes back and scratches at your door, pretend you're not home.

Therefore, rid yourselves of all malice.

1 PETER 2:1

EXERCISE MY RIGHT TO WRITE IN MY BIBLE

TO GET THE MOST OUT OF STUDYING THE BIBLE, YOU NEED THE UNITE STUFF!

Reading the Bible should be an interactive experience. As you read, think about how to apply God's words to your life. Write down action steps you plan to take. Underline passages you want to memorize. Highlight portions you are confused about and remind yourself to ask someone about them. The power of God's words does not reside in the impressive leather binding or the gilded edges of the pages, but in their ability to sink into your thoughts and soul.

If you still feel awkward about marking up your Bible, buy a notebook and use it to chronicle your thoughts and responses to God's life instruction manual and personal love letter.

If you are serious about your faith, put it in writing.

TAYLOR MORGAN

IF I REALLY WANTED TO
GROW CLOSER TO GOD,
I WOULD . . .

AVOID BEING A PEW POTATO

Being a pew potato leads to a half-baked spiritual life.

Are you a pew potato? A religious russet? A spiritual spud? Do you merely sit in church week after week, letting the messages and music slide through your ears without making an impression on your brain or your heart?

If so, it's time for a change. Actively *listen* to your pastor's words. Think about how you can apply them to your life—immediately. If the pastor brings up a wrong you are struggling with, ask for forgiveness right away. If you are reminded of the struggles of a family member or friend, make a note to pray for that person or write a letter of encouragement. The point is: do something, anything. Don't just sit there, get spiritually active.

It's great to have your feet on the ground, but keep them moving.

American Proverb

PRAY THE LORD'S PRAYER EVERY DAY

Make the Lord's Prayer your prayer as well.

So great is God's love for us that He even taught us what to pray. So on those days you're not sure what to say to your Father, open up your Bible and follow Jesus' model. Better yet, memorize this prayer (if you haven't already).

Be careful though that you don't let the words become rote, ritualized, and meaningless. After every few words you pray, think about what they mean. Ask yourself, "Did I truly mean what I just said?" If the answer is "no," pray the words again. Another way to keep the Lord's Prayer fresh and vibrant in your life is to read or memorize it in several different Bible versions.

Our Father in heaven, hallowed he your name, your kingdom come, your will he done on earth as it is in heaven. Give us today our daily bread. Forgive us our debts, as we also have forgiven our debtors. And lead us not into temptation, but deliver us from the evil one.

Matthew 6:9-13

Hold a Baby in My Arms

THANKS TO GOD'S GREAT LOVE,
WE NEED NEVER SAY, "BUT YOU
DON'T KNOW WHAT IT'S LIKE
DOWN HERE."

When people think of God, they tend to think of the Red Sea-parting, earthquake-making God. And awesome power is certainly part of who He is. But God also revealed Himself in the form of a helpless baby born in a manger 2,000 years ago. So the next time you hold a baby in your arms, imagine the Ruler of the Universe crying in hunger or shivering from the cold.

God could have come to earth as a full-grown, powerful man or a super-human hero. But He deliberately chose a harder, more humble road—a road that would be like the one we walk. Thus, He knows our experiences, our emotions, our humanity.

God's gifts put man's best dreams to shame.

ELIZABETH BARRETT BROWNING

If I really wanted to
grow closer to God,
I would . . .

Practice more Walk, Less Talk

A GOOD EXAMPLE IS THE BEST SERMON.

A recent newspaper feature told of an episode of "road rage." The driver of a compact car cut in front of a pickup truck during rush hour. The pickup driver honked at the compact and hollered a few angry words. The other driver screamed back, made an obscene gesture, and sped away. The noteworthy part of this story is that the compact car was tattooed with Christian bumper stickers, including one that read, "WHAT WOULD JESUS DO?"

It's one thing to talk about how you are drawing closer to God or proclaim it with stickers and posters. It's another matter to live as God would want you to, even in the heat of rush hour.

Go unto all the world and preach the Gospel.
Use words if necessary.

ST. FRANCIS

BE
PROUD
OF HIM

YOU CAN'T BE CLOSE TO HIM ON THE INSIDE IF YOU ARE AFRAID TO ACKNOWLEDGE HIM ON THE OUTSIDE.

We are proud of our children, our yards, our cars, our achievements. We are eager to display them to others and to extol their many fine qualities. But it's sometimes a different story with God. We are afraid to identify ourselves as His children because we fear we will be criticized—or labeled as religious fanatics.

The next time you feel a sense of embarrassment over your desire to grow closer to God, ask yourself, "What do I have to be ashamed of?" After all, God is creative and powerful. He is loving. He is merciful. He is the perfect Father, and His children should be the proudest offspring in the world.

Whoever acknowledges me before men, I will also acknowledge him before my Father in heaven. But whoever disowns me before men, I will disown him before my Father in heaven.

MATTHEW 10:32-33

IF I REALLY WANTED TO
GROW CLOSER TO GOD,
I WOULD . . .

PRACTICE PATIENCE

A HANDFUL OF PATIENCE IS BETTER THAN A BUCKETFUL OF BRAINS.

Patience is part of God's character. If you want to grow closer to Him, you must cultivate and nourish it in your life. So the next time you're stuck in traffic or in a long, slow moving supermarket line, say to yourself, "I'm not going to let this situation get to me. I'm going to practice patience." Then use the time to pray for someone—how about the person testing your patience, for example?

Practicing patience with people and situations will help you better appreciate how patient God is with your own imperfections and mistakes. It will cause you to feel close to Him.

One moment of patience may ward off great disaster.

CHINESE PROVERB

PUT AWAY THE SUPERMAN (OR SUPERWOMAN) CAPE

PUT AWAY THAT SUPERHERO CAPE. IT DOESN'T GO WITH WHAT YOU'RE WEARING.

Have you noticed how none of the TV or comic-book superheroes ever pray or go to church? Perhaps these individuals feel they don't need God. For us mortals, however, it's a different story. When you try to be a superhero and tackle life with your own human powers, you weaken your relationship with God.

Why? Because only when you admit you are weak can you experience His strength. Only when you acknowledge that you are sick can you know His healing. Only when you realize that you need His help, can you receive the help you need. So put your spirit of independence aside, and let Him meet your need.

The men who really believe in themselves are all in lunatic asylums.

G. K. CHESTERTON

Determine to Respect and Obey God's Rules of Right Living

AN OUNCE OF PREVENTION IS WORTH A POUND OF PURITY.

Farmers have a saying that goes, "Once you're standing in the pig pen, it's too late to worry about soiling your Sunday clothes." And that advice carries beyond the farm. How can you grow close to God if you are busy doing those things that hurt Him, hurt you, and hurt others?

God has given us a code of conduct to live by. In the same way you would steer your child away from danger, these injunctions to right living are intended to steer you out of harm's way. Determine right now to resist those things that are contrary to God's rules of right living, and commit to avoid settings in which you'll likely face temptation.

I have hidden your word in my heart that I might not sin against you.

PSALM 119:11

HONOR
MY
SPOUSE

DIVORCE YOURSELF FROM ANYTHING THAT COMES BETWEEN YOU AND YOUR SPOUSE.

God could have used any number of analogies to illustrate His relationship with His followers: employer/employee, teacher/student, even master/slave. But the one He chose was groom/bride. Clearly, the relationship between husband and wife is important to Him.

So, when you praise, compliment, care for, and celebrate your spouse, you are honoring a relationship God Himself created—and you understand better how much God cherishes those who respond to His love and care. If you are single, the Bible says that God Himself will look after you as a husband. Direct your praises His way, and you will be, of all, the most blessed.

Successful marriage is always a triangle: a man,
a woman, and God.

CECIL MYERS

DISCOVER GOD'S PURPOSE FOR MY LIFE

HAPPINESS IS KNOWING WHAT YOU WERE MEANT TO BE.

D o you have a sense of wonder about what you do in life? For example, if you're a teacher, are you merely downloading a bunch of facts upon your students or inspiring them with the thrill of learning? Is teaching just a job or is it a calling?

If what you do is just a job, you may have missed God's purpose for your life. Think of the first disciples Jesus called. They left all that they had to follow Him. Their hearts pounded with anticipation. Yours should as well. God's plan is for you to experience an abundant, vibrant life in perfect harmony with the gifts and callings He has placed in you. Find those and you will be one step closer to Him.

The purposes of the Almighty are perfect, and must prevail, though we erring mortals may fail to accurately perceive them in advance.

ABRAHAM LINCOLN

PRACTICE HUMILITY

THOSE WHO SING THEIR OWN PRAISES USUALLY SING SOLO.

We live in a day in which those with political clout, wealth, beauty, and fame occupy the "Most Admired" lists. God's standards are different. Think of Jesus' parables. The last shall be first, and the first last. A small seed becomes a great tree. One lost sheep takes priority over the rest of the flock.

The Bible defines faith as walking humbly before God. And as we walk this way, practicing humility, we become more in tune with the character of a God who left heaven to become a vulnerable human. Someone who was so humble that He even made Himself subject to a humiliating and painful death—for our sake.

The fear of the Lord teaches a man wisdom,
and humility comes before honor.

PROVERBS 15:33

REMEMBER THAT HE IS ALWAYS WITH ME

GOD IS ALWAYS JUST A PRAYER AWAY.

God cannot be contained in a building or a book. Yet we somehow forget Him unless we are in church or reading the Bible. Sometimes, in the midst of life's daily "busyness," we stop communicating with Him. Instead, our attention is on our computer screen, our checkbook, or the cars ahead of us in the traffic jam.

Don't allow life's details to turn your attention from your Creator. In the midst of your labor and duties, come to recognize that God is always right there with you—to hear you and to speak to you. His temple is always as close as your heart, waiting for you to enter and be refreshed and inspired.

Where love is, there is God also.

LEO TOLSTOY

IF I REALLY WANTED TO
GROW CLOSER TO GOD,
I WOULD . . .

REST

TO MAINTAIN GOOD RECEPTION, YOU MUST KEEP YOUR BATTERIES CHARGED.

God doesn't sweat. He doesn't get tired. He doesn't struggle with aching muscles after a day of hard work. Yet the Bible says that when He finished creating the world, He rested. If our all-powerful God took the time to rest, that should speak volumes to us mere mortals.

You need to rest occasionally. You need to recover physically, emotionally, and spiritually from life's demands. And in resting, you will find the time and the right frame of mind to contemplate God's wonders and to thank Him for His grace and kindness to you. You will also gather the energy to run the next miles on your journey with Him, and toward Him.

Even the best racehorse has to stop for oats once in awhile.

T. J. BOWER

IF I REALLY WANTED TO
GROW CLOSER TO GOD,
I WOULD . . .

WORK ON MY DEFENSE

IT DOESN'T MATTER WHAT YOU BELIEVE UNTIL YOU KNOW WHY YOU BELIEVE IT.

If you were called into court and asked to defend God's existence and purpose, could you do it? Could you craft a compelling case to support your beliefs?

The Bible tells us to be ready to give a thoughtful, reasonable defense for the hope that is in us. So if you want to be closer to God, it's important to know why you believe that He exists at all and be able to support it intellectually. In the process of building a strong defense for your faith, you'll become more confident in your heart and mind that God does exist and wants to be personally involved in your life.

Always be prepared to give an answer to everyone who asks you to give the reason for the hope that you have.

1 PETER 3:15

Give to Those in Need

YOU CAN NEVER OUT-GIVE GOD.

In one of His most compelling messages, Jesus taught that when we help the sick, the poor, the imprisoned, we help Him. He didn't say that it's like we're helping Him. He said, "I tell you the truth, whatever you did for one of the least of these brothers of mine, you did for me" (Matthew 25:40).

Thus, you must see Jesus in the hungry faces of third world children, the hopeless eyes of the street beggar, even the hardened expression of the convict. And as you see and give to Jesus by giving to those in need, you will be better able to appreciate all that He has given to you.

Do all the good you can,
By all the means you can,
In all the ways you can,
In all the places you can,
At all the times you can,
To all the people you can,
As long as ever you can.

JOHN WESLEY

EXPLORE
THE
CHRISTIAN
CLASSICS

FEED YOUR MIND AND SPIRIT: READ THE CLASSICS.

Want to be a good parent? Watch and learn from parents who are raising fulfilled, happy children. Want to be a good coach? Find one with a winning record and a team that respects him or her and competes with skill, maturity, and class.

But what about improving your spiritual life? Drawing closer to God? One way to accomplish this goal is to read the Christian classics. People like George MacDonald, C. S. Lewis, Martin Luther, and Charles Sheldon have honestly and eloquently written about many areas of Christian life and the challenges of growing closer to God. Their wisdom and inspiration are only a trip to the bookstore away.

Christian literature has some best sellers, hut even more blessed sellers.

TAYLOR MORGAN

IF I REALLY WANTED TO
GROW CLOSER TO GOD,
I WOULD . . .

REMEMBER
TO SAY,
"THANK YOU!"

GRATITUDE IS THE KEY TO HAPPINESS!

Thanksgiving Day has been set aside as a time to thank God for our blessings. But if you are serious about growing closer to God, you shouldn't wait until you are gnawing on a turkey leg or stuffing yourself with dressing to thank God for all He has done.

Whenever you feel God's hand on your life, let Him know. When you see Him working in the lives of those around you, thank Him for that too. And don't worry if you're sometimes unsure how to express your deep gratitude for His goodness. Just thank Him the best way you can. He'll get the message. After all, He's God.

Thanks be to God for his indescribable gift!

2 CORINTHIANS 9:15

IF I REALLY WANTED TO
GROW CLOSER TO GOD,
I WOULD . . .

LAUGH
MORE

LAUGHTER IS GOOD MEDICINE, AND IT'S AVAILABLE WITHOUT A PRESCRIPTION.

If you are a parent, uncle or aunt, teacher, baby-sitter, or coach, you know the pure joy that comes from hearing a child's laughter—especially if you had something to do with inspiring it. God invented laughter in order to nourish our souls. The Bible even records people using humor. Remember Elijah satirically taunting the prophets of Baal? Or Jesus' memorable words, "You strain out a gnat and swallow a camel"?

God always intended for us to enjoy His gift of laughter. So the next time you hear a funny story from the pulpit, a joke, or humorous song, don't rein in your laughter. Unleash it. Chances are, God is smiling, or even laughing right along with you.

I believe God loves to hear His children laugh.
What healthy father doesn't?

MARK LOWRY

IF I REALLY WANTED TO
GROW CLOSER TO GOD,
I WOULD . . .

LOVE
MY
ENEMIES

ENEMIES ARE MADE, NOT BORN.

I s there any tougher commandment than the one to love our enemies? Not tolerate them or simply do kind things for them. Love them. Those obnoxious, cruel, hateful people—yeah, right!

The first step to loving your enemies is praying for them (not for their humiliation or destruction, by the way). And when you pray for your enemies, pray as much for your own attitudes and behaviors as for theirs. That way, even if your prayers don't change your enemies' ugly qualities, they will change yours. And as you experience what hard work it is to love unlovable people, you will value God's love more than ever.

You have heard that it was said, "Love your neighbor and hate your enemy." But I tell you: Love your enemies and pray for those who persecute you.

MATTHEW 5:43-44

IF I REALLY WANTED TO
GROW CLOSER TO GOD,
I WOULD . . .

APPROACH SOMEONE UN-APPROACHABLE

WHAT WE DO FOR THE DOWNTRODDEN, THE OUTCASTS WE ENCOUNTER, IS WHAT WE DO FOR JESUS.

In Jesus' time, Jews were legally forbidden to associate with the likes of beggars, tax collectors, and prostitutes. So when He befriended such people, Jesus didn't merely smash social and cultural barriers, He broke the law. And He didn't just spout Scriptures to these people. He ate with them. He touched them.

That's why it's so important for you to remember that the street beggars, drunks, and derelicts you encounter are loved by God as much as you are. And how you respond to them, how you treat them, is the true measure of your relationship with the heavenly Father.

They say, "Here is a glutton and a drunkard, a friend of tax collectors and 'sinners.'" But wisdom is proved right by her actions.

MATTHEW 11:19

If I Really Wanted to Grow Closer to God, I Would . . .

Slow Down to Pray

THE BIRDS THAT FLY HIGHEST ARE THE BIRDS OF "PRAY."

Are your prayers quick monologues to God or conversations *with* God? Prayer is as much about listening to Him as it is speaking to Him. Often, we hit God with a barrage of requests, utter a few halfhearted "thank you's," then hurry on to the next order of the day. That is not prayer.

True prayer is unhurried. It's communication with your heavenly Father, the Creator of the universe. So slow down. Enter His presence in quietness and reverence. Pay attention to the words and feelings you get from Him as you pray. And let your prayers take as long as they need to take. Focus on communication rather than agendas, schedules, or limits.

If you haven't got the time to talk to God, you don't have a prayer.

OLIVIA KENT

Realize that Intimacy with Him takes Time

GROWING IN PERSONAL RELATIONSHIP WITH GOD IS A MARATHON, NOT A FORTY-YARD DASH.

We live in an age of immediate gratification, with its instant coffee, Minute Rice, and microwave dinners. Even first-class mail is now called "snail mail." We must realize that there is no instant formula for intimacy with God. Some have sought it, only to give up in discouragement.

Relationships take time. And the very idea of growing closer to God evokes a process: learning more about Him, growing more aware of His presence in your life, and becoming more confident in His love and power. So take the time to get to know God. And leave the instant gratification to the coffee people.

And Jesus grew in wisdom and stature, and in favor with God and men.

LUKE 2:52

STRIVE TO BE A SAINT, NOT A CELEBRITY

THE WORLD HAS ENOUGH CELEBRITIES. IT COULD USE A FEW MORE SAINTS.

To some, life is a theater in which they play the role of celebrity. They flaunt their talents and accomplishments, even their super-spirituality. They are like the Pharisees of Jesus' day, who made a big production even out of fasting. They wanted everyone to be impressed by their long, hungry faces.

All people do this in one way or another, lurking behind masks that cloak their insecurities or hide selfish agendas. The walk of faith is no place for masks. It's a place for naked faces, blemishes and all. A place where people look each other in the eye, and look to God for guidance, hope, and forgiveness.

For whoever exalts himself will he humbled, and whoever humbles himself will be exalted.

MATTHEW 23:12

Remember that Heaven is a Real Place

WHAT'S AHEAD OF US IS FAR BETTER THAN ANYTHING THAT'S BEHIND US.

A young man completing a job application came to the line asking for his "permanent address." He thought for a moment, then wrote "Heaven." He understood that heaven is a real place—and ultimately, it will be his home and the home of all those who put their trust in God.

You will be more conscious of God in your everyday life if you remember—like the young man—that He is the landlord of your permanent home. Someday you will actually meet Him. How you will feel about that experience depends on how you spend your time here in your temporary home—earth.

The world has forgotten, in its concern with Left and Right, that there is an Above and Below.

GLEN DRAKE

IF I REALLY WANTED TO
GROW CLOSER TO GOD,
I WOULD . . .

STOP
SWEATING
THE SMALL
STUFF

WORRY IS THE INTEREST PAID BY THOSE WHO BORROW TROUBLE.

It's amazing how minor irritations can take our eyes off God. Tension headaches interrupt our sleep. Telemarketers interrupt our dinner. Car troubles interrupt our vacations. At times like these, we must step back and regain perspective. What is a traffic ticket or flat tire or cold sore compared with being loved purely and eternally by almighty God?

Take your worries to God in prayer and leave them there. If you find that difficult to do, remember that you are entrusting your cares to the One who hung the stars and set the planets in motion, the One who created the earth and all that is in it. He should be able to handle whatever you bring before Him.

Who of you by worrying can add a single hour to his life?

MATTHEW 6:27

IF I REALLY WANTED TO
GROW CLOSER TO GOD,
I WOULD . . .

STOP HOLDING OUT ON HIM

TO BE HOLY, YOU MUST BE WHOLLY HIS.

To be near God, you don't have to be perfect. But there is one requirement: you must totally submit yourself to Him. That means nothing held back—unconditional surrender. Just as you can't be "mostly married" or "somewhat pregnant," you cannot think of God as a "nodding acquaintance." Relationship with God simply doesn't work that way.

If you choose to hang onto some area of your life, will God still love you? Of course! He loved you long before you were even aware of Him. But, if you truly want to grow close to God, to know Him as a friend, you must give yourself completely into His care.

Give, and it will be given to you. A good measure, pressed down, shaken together and running over, will be poured into your lap. For with the measure you use, it will be measured to you.

LUKE 6:38

IF I REALLY WANTED TO
GROW CLOSER TO GOD,
I WOULD . . .

OPEN
MY
HEART

A HEART OPEN TO GOD IS A HEART OPEN TO GOOD.

Life's pain and disappointment can cause us to close our hearts tight like a fist. Or we may close our hearts to hold on to something we fear losing. Unfortunately, a tense heart can't relax, can't laugh, can't truly love. And it can't fully receive God's love.

An open heart signals a readiness for whatever changes, surprises, and gifts God has to offer. Picture your heart as a door—a door that you can leave open for God. After all, He is the One who built the door and the house. And He has already made it clear that He wants to come in and stay with you forever.

Paradise is open to all receptive hearts.

OLIVIA KENT

IF I REALLY WANTED TO GROW CLOSER TO GOD, I WOULD . . .

TRAVEL LIGHT

THE EXCESS BAGGAGE OF MATERIALISM ALWAYS MAKES THE JOURNEY MORE DIFFICULT.

Many Americans have a possession obsession—laptop computers, digital TVs, cell phones, sports cars. These items aren't inherently bad, but they can easily become sources of security, even of pride.

Jesus taught His followers to travel light. To take with them only what they would need for their journey. He reminded them to concentrate on the grace of His Spirit—and not to be distracted by the glitter of shiny things. Why? Because the light of God's divine love is so brilliant that it makes everything else pale in comparison. If you want to really know Him, don't get distracted by worldly possessions.

Whoever loves money never has money enough; whoever loves wealth is never satisfied with his income.

ECCLESIASTES 5:10

Remember
that it
Pays to
Praise

OUR PRAISE IS ONE OF GOD'S FAVORITE PLACES TO BE.

One of the Bible's most reassuring promises is found in Psalm 22:3, which says that God inhabits the praise of His people. This is a rather mysterious concept, but we can be confident that when we praise God, when we commend Him, when we express our esteem for Him, somehow His presence is there.

So come closer to God. Adore Him. Thank Him. Praise Him. Celebrate Him. Worship Him in whatever way best expresses what's in your heart. Talk to Him. Sing to Him. Or lift your eyes toward heaven and simply smile at Him. And He will be there with you.

Doth not all nature around me praise God? If I were silent, I should be an exception to the universe.

CHARLES H. SPURGEON

IF I REALLY WANTED TO GROW CLOSER TO GOD, I WOULD . . .

KEEP A SPIRITUAL JOURNAL

A SPIRITUAL JOURNAL IS A GREAT WAY TO CHRONICLE YOUR SPIRITUAL JOURNEY.

Your relationship with God is worth writing home about. Record your thoughts, discoveries, applications, questions, goals. Putting these things in writing helps make them more tangible—and probably easier to remember. Another benefit of the spiritual journal is that you can look back on it and note the progress you've made in your relationship with God. You can see how He's made clear what once was confusing. And you can recall how He has answered your prayers.

When you want someone to stand behind a promise or statement he has made, you may say, "Put it in writing." If you value your relationship with God, do likewise.

The only important thing a writer needs is a subject.

BROOKS ATKINSON

IF I REALLY WANTED TO
GROW CLOSER TO GOD,
I WOULD . . .

ADMIRE HIS CREATION

THE UNIVERSE IS GOD'S WORK OF ART, AND WORK OF HEART.

J ust as the vision, passion, and talent of a great painter can be seen in his art, God has revealed Himself to us through His creation. We should allow ourselves to be awed and moved by the intricacy, wonder, and beauty of God's handiwork. The expanse of the sky filled with stars. The vastness of the oceans. The marvel of the human body.

And remember, the all-powerful Master Creator of the universe loves you and wants to have a personal relationship with you. He desires it so much that He has painted a magnificent masterpiece in His creation to draw you to His side.

The heavens declare the glory of God; the skies proclaim the work of his hands.

PSALM 19:1

SAY "PHOOEY" TO FEAR

IF YOU FIND YOUR KNEES KNOCKING, KNEEL ON THEM.

God is an authority figure, and some of us fear authority figures. We may picture an angry father or a harsh teacher or coach. Perhaps one of these people abused his or her power, we've never forgotten it, and now we're afraid to get too close to God. We remember the wounds of the past. We're not sure we can ever trust again.

If that is where you find yourself, fear not! God will not betray you, disappoint you, or abuse you. Remember what He did for you. He has proven His love and trustworthiness. No one who has trusted God and become close to Him has ever been disappointed.

Do the thing that you fear, and the death of fear is certain.

AMERICAN PROVERB

Heed His Correction

GOD'S CORRECTION IS ALWAYS CORRECT.

The Bible notes that God reproves those He loves. He isn't out to ruin us or make us pay. He simply wants to protect us from the disasters our willfulness often creates. How does He correct us? We may hear His voice speaking deep within, through our consciences. Or God may urge someone to speak a word of truth to us. He also attempts to steer us back on course by allowing us to suffer the consequences of our actions.

However they come to you, God's reproofs are like mirrors, reminding you when your face is dirty and needs cleaning. Take a look. And if you see something that needs fixing, with God's help—fix it.

Whoever heeds correction is honored.

PROVERBS 13:18

IF I REALLY WANTED TO
GROW CLOSER TO GOD,
I WOULD . . .

MEMORIZE A VERSE A WEEK

ASK GOD TO HELP YOU RECALL SCRIPTURES, AND DON'T FORGET TO SAY, "THANKS FOR THE MEMORIES."

You probably won't have a Bible at your fingertips every moment of your life. But you can have God's wisdom "at the ready" if you commit to memorizing just one verse a week. You may think you're not good at memorizing, but you can probably recite a few key verses already—not to mention the "Pledge of Allegiance" and most of the words to "The Star-Spangled Banner."

As you memorize each verse, think about its implications, how you might apply it in everyday life. Armed with God's Word in your mind and heart, you'll feel much closer to God and better prepared to make wise choices.

I used to have trouble memorizing stuff, before I read that book by what's his name.

DREW CODY
(IN THE STAND-UP GUY)

IF I REALLY WANTED TO
GROW CLOSER TO GOD,
I WOULD . . .

READ
CHRISTIAN
MAGAZINES

IT'S WORTH CHECKING OUT THE MAGAZINE SCENE.

If you've passed by a newsstand recently, you've probably noticed the variety of magazines available. Whether you're a scuba diver, chocolate lover, or dirt-bike rider, there's a magazine for you.

But what you may not know is that there are dozens of Christian magazines tailored to a variety of interests. You can read about Christian music, Christian athletes, or Christian media personalities. There are even magazines for worship leaders and biblical archaeology buffs. Take the time to investigate what's available. You'll probably find a publication that addresses your passion for your hobby or area of interest—and your passion for God.

Finally, brothers, whatever is true, whatever is noble, whatever is right, whatever is pure, whatever is lovely, whatever is admirable—if anything is excellent or praiseworthy—think about such things.

PHILIPPIANS 4:8

Avoid Screening God's Calls

SCREENING OUT GOD CAN LEAVE YOU SPIRITUALLY EMPTY.

We spend much of our lives in front of screens. Computer screens, TV screens, smartphone screens. Some of this screen time is unavoidable, but think about how much time you can waste in front of various screens. A little internet scrolling can subtly turn into hours that leave you with little more than glazed eyes and sore buns.

What's worse, screen time can gobble up hours that could be put to better use—time with God, family, or friends. Time is one of the most valuable possessions you will ever have. Don't waste it. Invest it in things of lasting value by committing to carefully screening your screen time.

He calls his own sheep by name.

JOHN 10:3

REMEMBER THAT GOD DID THE CHOOSING

If God didn't choose, we'd lose.

Remember the thrill of being picked first for a sports team? Or the agony of being picked last—or ending up on a team purely by default? One of the beautiful things about a life in close relationship with God is knowing that we have been chosen first for His team.

God chose you long before you chose Him—before you decided that you wanted to be close to Him. In fact, the Bible says that He chose you even before the foundations of the earth were set in place. That's right! God chose you first, and even the little prodding in your heart that made you want to know Him, came from Him. Even your faith is His gift.

For he [God] chose us in him before the creation of the world to be holy and blameless in his sight.

Ephesians 1:4

If I really wanted to Grow Closer to God, I would . . .

Treat my Body like a Temple, Not a Bowling Alley

GUARDING YOUR HEALTH SHOWS RESPECT FOR YOUR CREATOR.

I f an esteemed guest came to live with you, what accommodations would you provide? Wouldn't you try to make your home as inviting and pleasant as possible? The Bible teaches that our bodies are the temples of God's Spirit. That means that as we grow close to God, eventually we invite Him to come and live within us—just as when a couple makes their vows of marriage and thereafter live together in the same house.

Is your temple an appropriate dwelling place for God? You don't have to be a model or an Olympic athlete, but your body is a gift from God. So honor Him by treating it right.

Activity strengthens. Inactivity weakens.

HIPPOCRATES

IF I REALLY WANTED TO
GROW CLOSER TO GOD,
I WOULD . . .

OBEY THE TEN COMMANDMENTS

GOD'S COMMANDMENTS ARE A PERFECT TEN.

Long before David Letterman, God created the original "Top Ten" list—His Ten Commandments. These rules for right living aren't allowed to be posted in some schools anymore, but they should be inscribed in our hearts and minds. The Ten Commandments are more than wise guidelines for living a holy and pleasing life; they also tell us much about God's character.

As you follow the Ten Commandments, you walk in step with their author, and His values become your values as well. Soon you will find yourself thinking like He thinks and doing what He would do. You will never know God completely—in many ways He is unknowable. But you can learn to walk by His side.

You shall have no other gods before me. You shall not make for yourself an idol . . . You shall not bow down to them or worship them . . . You shall not misuse the name of the Lord your God—Remember the Sabbath day by keeping it holy . . . Honor your father and your mother . . . You shall not murder. You shall not commit adultery. You shall not steal. You shall not give false testimony against your neighbor. You shall not covet.

EXODUS 20:3-17

IF I REALLY WANTED TO
GROW CLOSER TO GOD,
I WOULD . . .

KEEP MY PROMISES TO HIM

YOUR RELATIONSHIP WITH GOD SHOULD HE BUILT ON PROMISES, NOT COMPROMISES.

Have you ever promised God you would do something—or stop doing something—then later forgotten about the promise or brushed it aside? Promises to a holy God shouldn't be taken lightly. Unkept promises create walls between us and our Creator, because we lose our confidence and draw back from His love and blessing.

So don't make vows to God without thinking them through very carefully. When you promise Him something, keep your promise. When you have learned to honor God in this way, you will find it much easier to keep your promises to the earth dwellers in your life.

We must not promise what we ought not, lest we be called to perform what we cannot.

ABRAHAM LINCOLN

TRULY WORSHIP HIM

WORSHIP IS TO THE CHRISTIAN LIFE WHAT THE MAINSPRING IS TO A WATCH.

True worship isn't about religious rituals, but rather the pure and genuine expression of praise from a willing and eager heart. Children have much to teach us in this regard. They come to us without agendas, without pretension, without motives. They come with true hearts. It is close to impossible to walk away untouched by these unfettered affirmations, and God finds our true worship equally as compelling.

Choose any method you like to worship God: singing, reading Scripture, praying aloud, or by simple and silent reverence—there are a limitless number of ways. No matter how you choose to go about it, remember to do so with the heart of a child.

The life of man consists in beholding God.

ST. IRENAEUS

Remember that God loves all his children

GOD'S HAND IS EXTENDED TO ALL MANKIND.

I t might be easy to believe that God loves you or Billy Graham or some other great leader, but what about that frightful-looking rock star or dishonest politician? Do you tend to believe that God must love you more than them?

God loves all His children, though He grieves over those who choose not to respond to His love and care. So the next time you see someone offensive to you, remember: God loves that person no less than He loves you, or Billy Graham, or one of the saints of old. If you want to be close to God, you must learn to love the unlovely.

In humility consider others better than your-selves.

PHILIPPIANS 2:3

REMEMBER THAT MONEY AND MATERIAL GOODS ARE IMMATERIAL

Remember, it's "In God We Trust," not "In Gold We Trust."

It's ironic that money carries the words "In God We Trust," because wealth—or the pursuit of it—can hinder our trust in God. Money and possessions can never truly satisfy the human soul. A guy named Solomon tried that route and was left empty.

Only God can establish your self-worth and fulfill your deepest longings. Only relationship with Him can make you alive to His love, aware of your life's purpose, and filled with inner peace. And unlike money, God will never disappear, be taken away, or lose His value. Remember that money may rule the world's economy but it takes a back seat in God's economy.

Money has never yet made anyone rich.

SENECA

IF I REALLY WANTED TO GROW CLOSER TO GOD, I WOULD . . .

USE MY TALENTS

DO WHAT YOU CAN WITH WHAT YOU'VE BEEN GIVEN.

God has given each of us abilities. If we develop these skills, we can then use them in a way that will benefit others and bring glory to our Creator. What about your skills? Are you using them? Or are they lying dormant, gathering dust?

Putting your God-given talents to work is one of the most satisfying things you can do. As you do what God created you to do, you gain a deep sense of purpose—and you become closer and more grateful to the One who gave you your talents. There are few things as beautiful as Creator and creation working hand in hand.

Abilities are like tax deductions—we either use them or we lose them.

SAM JENNINGS

Be Willing to Search for Him

WE MAY NO LONGER RIDE CAMELS, BUT WISE MEN AND WOMEN STILL SEEK GOD.

The wise men's friends must have questioned if they were really wise. Here were these fellows, following only hearsay and one bright star on a long journey—a journey filled with unanswered questions and many risks. But their long search was rewarded when they found the child king, offered their gifts, and expressed their deep and humble adoration.

Even today, the wise men can be our guides, our examples. Their story can be your story. Are you willing to take the journey—whether physical, intellectual, or spiritual—that will lead you into God's presence?

We saw his star in the east and have come to worship him.

MATTHEW 2:2

IF I REALLY WANTED TO
GROW CLOSER TO GOD,
I WOULD . . .

LISTEN TO CHRISTIAN MUSIC

CHRISTIAN MUSIC CAN BRING US INTO HARMONY WITH GOD.

Today's Christian music offers something for every taste—from classical to hip-hop to heavy metal. But regardless of their musical style, Christian artists have a common purpose: to glorify God through their music, to celebrate life, and to share some of their most honest moments before God. Some artists have revealed that when they are recording, they feel a deep and real sense of God's anointing.

You can share in that anointing as you share in their music. Visit a bookstore and choose something in harmony with your own personal taste. And then, take some time to listen up and let your soul soar!

The Lord is my strength and my song.

PSALM 118:14

CELEBRATE MY INDIVIDUALITY

GOD'S CHILDREN ARE FEARFULLY AND WONDERFULLY FORMED IN THEIR MOTHERS' WOMBS, NOT MASS-PRODUCED ON AN ASSEMBLY LINE.

God didn't make you like anyone else on the entire planet. Even identical twins aren't truly identical. God made you unique, and He has unique plans for you and your talents—and even your limitations.

That's why you must never put yourself down because you are not like everyone else. Instead revel in your individuality and thank your Creator who had the inspiration and foresight to make you exactly the way you are. You are special because He has made you so, and understanding that will draw you closer to Him.

I thank God for my handicaps, for, through them, I have found myself, my work, and my God.

HELEN KELLER

IF I REALLY WANTED TO
GROW CLOSER TO GOD,
I WOULD . . .

THINK
SMALL

LITTLE THINGS MAKE A BIG DIFFERENCE TO GOD.

Our world loves bigness. Large, economy-sized boxes of detergent. Super-sized meals. Vehicles with extra leg room and extra head room. God is certainly capable of big feats. He parted the Red Sea. He created the universe in less than a week. But He also used only a small army to defeat the Midianites and fed a whole multitude of people from one boy's small lunch. And He sent a tiny baby to save the world.

Don't measure your success by how well-known you are or how much money you have. God isn't impressed with your bigness. He is interested in your life and the small but faithful steps you take toward Him each day.

Who despises the day of small things?

ZECHARIAH 4:10

REMEMBER THAT I DON'T LOOK GOOD IN GREEN

GOD'S CHILDREN SHOULD BE ZEALOUS, NOT JEALOUS.

God hates jealousy so much that He mentioned it in two of His Ten Commandments. We are all God's creation. He loves us all, and we shouldn't compare our "blessings" with those of others. When we envy what others have, we rob ourselves of the joy and contentment we should find in what God has given us.

Guard your heart. If you find that you are unable to rejoice over the success of others, beware. Instead of focusing on what others have, ask God to remind you of the many blessings He has given you—and how many of them are undeserved.

Envy takes the joy, happiness, and contentment out of living.

BILLY GRAHAM

IF I REALLY WANTED TO
GROW CLOSER TO GOD,
I WOULD . . .

LEARN TO TAKE "NO" FOR AN ANSWER

GOD'S ANSWER ISN'T ALWAYS YES, BUT IT IS ALWAYS PERFECT.

God is not Santa Claus. Nor is He a heavenly vending machine that dispenses goodies on demand. God doesn't give us all we ask for. Remember, Jesus' prayer to have the cup of death taken from Him? Even Christ Himself didn't get affirmative answers to all of His prayers.

Remember that God does *hear* every prayer, but He may decide it is best not to answer in the way you hope He will. Be open-hearted at these times. You may learn more about God and His will for your life from the "no" and "wait" answers than you do from the times He provides exactly what you ask for.

God always answers prayer, but His answer isn't always, "yes."

OLIVIA KENT

AVOID RELYING ON EMOTIONS

GOD'S LOVE IS MORE THAN A FEELING; IT'S A FACT.

E motions are wonderful. They add flavor and heat to life. They make us feel more alive. Emotions, however, make lousy foundations for our faith in God because they can be radically affected by things like diet, lack of sleep, and internal chemistry. You shouldn't look to your feelings to judge whether God loves You. Your assurance isn't from getting goose bumps or chills down your spine—after all, the flu can provide that.

Thank God that His love for us isn't based on how we *feel*; it's based on His integrity. His promises remain true regardless of how we feel about them.

Now faith is being sure of what we hope for
and certain of what we do not see.

HEBREWS 11:1

REMEMBER THAT I'M PART OF HIS RELAY TEAM

DON'T FORGET TO KEEP THE MEMORY OF GOD ALIVE.

One responsibility of a close relationship with God is to pass on to others the wisdom and inspiration you receive from your walk with Him. Just as you will almost certainly benefit from the encouragement of those who have walked with God before you, now you must run your relay leg with vigor and care—then pass on the memory of God in your life to others.

If you don't do your part, that memory will fade, and future generations will be deprived of a sense of history and knowledge of God's faithfulness to those who seek Him and find Him throughout the ages.

We have received the baton of faith. We must pass it carefully on to the next generation.

TAYLOR MORGAN

IF I REALLY WANTED TO
GROW CLOSER TO GOD,
I WOULD . . .

STOP WORRYING AND BE HOPEFUL

TURN YOUR WORRIES OVER TO GOD, AND LET HIS PERFECT PEACE GUIDE YOUR HEART.

In Philippians 4, Paul instructs us to "be anxious for *nothing*." Think about that. Paul says the child of God shouldn't worry about anything! And Paul didn't give this advice lightly. He was in prison at the time he wrote it. But despite all his trials, Paul knew God could bring peace. God doesn't always untie all the knots in our lives. But He does give us the grace to live with the knots.

So remember, there is nothing you face that is too difficult, too troubling, or too frightening for God. He holds the world in the palm of His hand. Your problems aren't likely to stump Him.

Worry is the misuse of the imagination.

ANONYMOUS

IF I REALLY WANTED TO
GROW CLOSER TO GOD,
I WOULD . . .

GO TO HIM IN TIMES OF TROUBLE

When you face trouble, go to God on the double.

Some of the closest relationships are forged in times of crisis—on the battlefield, in the hospital, or during a natural disaster. Yet many people run from God—out of anger or despair—when calamity occurs, forfeiting a wonderful opportunity to grow closer to Him.

If you're tempted to flee from God in times of trouble, know that He never loses control of any situation. He knows what He is doing or allowing to happen. So once You have found Him, don't leave His protection. Cling to your fellowship with Him. Remember, every good father wants his children to rely on him when pain and disaster strike.

God is our refuge and strength, a very present help in trouble.

Psalm 46:1 KJV

IF I REALLY WANTED TO
GROW CLOSER TO GOD,
I WOULD . . .

LET GO
OF PAST
FAILURES

GLORY ISN'T IN NEVER FAILING, BUT IN RISING EVERY TIME YOU FALL.

As imperfect people, we make mistakes. We drop the ball, miss the mark, fall on our faces, use too many cliches. Failure can make us feel inadequate, especially when we compare ourselves to others who seem to be living more effectively.

When you feel like a failure compared to others, remember your proper motivation for life: You have chosen to live in close fellowship with God out of your love for Him rather than to impress an audience of your peers. Focus on God, and know that He will cheer you on—and pick you up and dust you off when you fall. And He won't hold your failures against you, so don't hold them against yourself.

The greatest failure is the failure to try.

WILLIAM WARD

WELCOME TRIALS

DON'T BE GUILTY OF GIVING TRIALS AN UNJUST VERDICT.

When athletes train hard, they run or lift weights to the point of muscle failure. This approach actually breaks down muscle fibers, which would seem to be a detriment to performance. However, it's beneficial because the body adapts to the stress and rebuilds the damaged fibers stronger than ever before.

This principle is also important to our spiritual strength and stamina. God does not cause our pain and struggle, but He does allow a certain amount of adversity to come into our lives. His purpose is to see that we grow strong and resilient rather than weak and complacent. So smile when you encounter trials. See them as opportunities to grow strong in your faith and closer to God.

In the presence of trouble, some grow wings.
Others buy crutches.

AMERICAN PROVERB

PUT AWAY MY GAVEL

SITTING HIGH IN THE JUDGMENT SEAT KEEPS YOU FROM GETTING ON YOUR KNEES.

Judges today are celebrities. Some even have their own television shows where they scold, cajole, and sentence those who come before them. Sometimes it's tempting to put on the long black robes ourselves and pass judgment on others. It's easy for us to see their faults and pronounce them "Guilty!" There's only one problem. Being judgmental is courting disaster.

When you pronounce verdicts on others, you open yourself up to the same kind of prosecution. So leave the judging to God. And when you see others misbehaving, thank God for His mercy, which is available to all and free for the asking.

Do not judge, or you too will be judged.

MATTHEW 7:1

If I really wanted to
grow closer to God,
I would . . .

Look in the Mirror and say, "Hello, Masterpiece."

GOD'S WORKS OF ART ARE BUILT FOR ACTION, NOT AUCTION.

Ephesians 2:10 tells us that we are "God's workmanship, created in Christ Jesus to do good works." That means we are God's works of art. Imagine that. You are the creation of the only perfect artist in the universe. And the news just keeps getting better. God didn't craft you merely to sit around collecting dust in some cosmic art gallery. He created you for a purpose—His purpose.

So next time your self-esteem takes a hit, and you think you aren't important enough, smart enough, sophisticated enough, charming enough, rich enough, or good- looking enough to draw close to God, remember who you are—God's work of art. God's *functional* work of art.

So God created man in his own image, in the image of God he created him, male and female he created them.

GENESIS 1:27

IF I REALLY WANTED TO
GROW CLOSER TO GOD,
I WOULD . . .

QUIT
TRYING TO
SHRINK
HIM

GOD DOESN'T FIT WELL IN SMALL BOXES OF HUMAN INVENTION.

Many people like to reduce God to something small and simple enough for their finite minds to understand. But God's ways are not our ways. And we can get so caught up in a destination called "Complete Understanding" that we forget to enjoy the journey.

Think of how many times Jesus answered a question with another question—or didn't deliver when people demanded, "Show us a sign!" Maybe He was trying to teach us something—that the search for God matters more than arriving at the mistaken notion that we've brought Him down to our level and captured His essence. Maybe it's the search itself that makes us who we are.

Your God is too small!

J. B. PHILLIPS

FLY WITH EAGLES RATHER THAN CRAWL WITH SLUGS

KEEP IN MIND THAT IT'S EASIER TO BE PULLED DOWN THAN TO BE PULLED UP.

Companionship choices are difficult. Jesus spent time with many people of low reputation. Yet the Bible cautions us that bad company corrupts good character. The key to following Jesus' example *and* protecting ourselves lies in discernment. Follow these simple guidelines.

First, spend as much time as possible with godly people who will encourage you to grow closer to God. Second, as you befriend troubled people, be careful to do so on your terms, as much as possible. And third, you must constantly ask yourself, "Am I drawing these people toward God, or are they drawing me away?"

He who walks with the wise grows wise, but a companion of fools suffers harm.

PROVERBS 13:20

IF I REALLY WANTED TO
GROW CLOSER TO GOD,
I WOULD . . .

BEGIN TO

APPRECIATE

HIS PASSIONS

WE STRIVE TO EMPATHIZE WITH FAMILY AND FRIENDS, WHY NOT ALSO WITH GOD?

God is not an emotionless robotic power. The Bible says that God has intense feelings—sorrow over those who choose to live without His love and joy over those who turn from their destructive paths. If you want to grow closer to God, ask Him to let you feel a part of what He feels.

Imagine what a privilege it would be to glimpse inside the holy and eternal heart of God. To feel His godly compassion for suffering humanity. To feel His righteous indignation for those who are treated unjustly. To feel His fatherly delight when one of His children hurries to spend time with Him. It would surely change your life.

The Lord is gracious and compassionate, slow to anger and rich in love.

PSALM 145:8

GO
TO
CHURCH

SORROWS ARE DIMINISHED AND JOYS MULTIPLIED WHEN YOU SHARE THEM.

I f you are serious about growing closer in your relationship with God, then it is vitally important that you find a church home where you feel comfortable and attend regularly. Meeting together with other believers provides encouragement and instruction as you walk the road of faith.

Once you find the right congregation, take time to get to know those you see every week. Take time to learn about the services and programs your church can provide. Get involved with the activities your church provides for church members and the community as a whole. You will be blessed by the support and comfort a church family can provide.

Let us not give up meeting together.

HEBREWS 10:25

IF I REALLY WANTED TO
GROW CLOSER TO GOD,
I WOULD . . .

RESPOND IMMEDIATELY TO HIS CALLINGS

THE TIME YOU KILL CAN NEVER HE RESUSCITATED.

The Bible tells us to "redeem the time" (Ephesians 5:16 KJV). That means that we should make the most of every opportunity, because some don't linger for long. So when we feel a prompting from our heavenly Father, we should never say, "Leave a message, and I'll get back to You later." Remember, God has legions of angels who will do whatever He asks. He wants us to share in His divine activity for *our* benefit, not His.

It's our loss when we miss the opportunity to serve Him. So respond immediately when you hear God speak. His will is perfect, and His plans for you always lead to abundant life.

What I mean, brothers, is that the time is short.

1 CORINTHIANS 7:29

REALIZE THERE IS NOWHERE HE WON'T GO

"Don't go there" is one of the most overused phrases of the late 1990s. But it doesn't apply to God. He never sends His children anywhere alone. In Old Testament times, He was with them as a pillar of fire, a cloud, a burning bush, or a voice from heaven. Today, He is with us in the form of His Holy Spirit, the Bible, and godly leaders and friends.

So, if you're enduring trials, remember that the Lord has gone before you and is also with you now. He knows what you are facing—He has even endured death—and He's ready to respond to your need.

If the Lord be with us, we have no cause of fear. His eye is upon us, His arm over us, His ear open to our prayer—His grace sufficient, His promise unchangeable.

JOHN NEWTON

Meditate on His Word

DON'T HESITATE TO MEDITATE.

Some people are frightened by the word meditation. It evokes images of bearded gurus sitting cross-legged in robes and chanting meaningless monosyllables. However, to meditate simply means to think deeply and continuously about something.

For the person who wants to grow closer to God, meditation can consist merely of focusing on the Bible's teachings and the God behind them. It's letting Him fill your mind and heart—and even the farthest corner of your soul. Meditate on God's goodness, on His wisdom and counsel, on His love and kindness. Meditate on His awesome creation and wondrous works. It doesn't matter what aspect of God you choose, meditating on Him will transform your life.

A man of meditation is happy, not for an hour or a day, but quite round the circle of all his years.

ISAAC TAYLOR

Dedicate my Efforts to Him

GIVE IT ALL YOU'VE GOT FOR GOD.

Legendary college football coach Knute Rockne gleaned a marvelous performance from his team one time by urging them to "win one for the Gipper," a deceased former player. How much more motivation can we muster by dedicating our efforts to the God who created us and loves us eternally.

Whether you're doing something athletic, artistic, or career-oriented, do it for God. Dedicate everything you do to God as a gesture of appreciation for the talents He has placed in your life. Then, however your efforts turn out, you will know the joy of pleasing and honoring Him.

Commit thy works unto the Lord, and thy thoughts shall he established.

PROVERBS 16:3 KJV

IF I REALLY WANTED TO
GROW CLOSER TO GOD,
I WOULD . . .

REMEMBER

TOO MANY PEOPLE HAVE SHORT MEMORIES AND LONG LISTS OF WANTS.

"You're only as good as your last game" is a popular adage in sports today. And a hit song a few years ago asked the question, "What have you done for me lately?" Look at the story of the Israelites in the Old Testament. They forgot about how God had parted the Red Sea and delivered them from their oppressors. A short while after that miraculous event, they were worshipping a golden statue of a calf.

It's important to remember all God has done for you—all the love, mercy, and answered prayers that have brought you to this point in your life. That same God will be with you in the future, and that means all of eternity.

When memory makes a journey into the past we live not once, but twice, the best times of our lives.

E. C. RAYBURN

IF I REALLY WANTED TO
GROW CLOSER TO GOD,
I WOULD . . .

CONCENTRATE ON BEING FAITHFUL, NOT SUCCESSFUL

IF AT FIRST YOU DON'T SUCCEED, BE FAITHFUL AND KEEP TRYING.

In contemporary society, people are judged by numbers—how much money they grossed last year, how many new clients they brought in. Given the world's view of success, it's easy to assume God thinks the same way. Thus, people sometimes focus on church attendance, number of volunteer activities, or the amount of money they put in the offering as the ways to please Him.

God is not some great statistician in the sky. He's more concerned with the state of your heart than how many good deeds you perform. So focus on simply being faithful to Him, and success will take care of itself.

Let love and faithfulness never leave you.

PROVERBS 3:3

IF I REALLY WANTED TO
GROW CLOSER TO GOD,
I WOULD . . .

BE
UNAFRAID
OF AGE

THERE ARE NONE SO OLD AS THOSE WHO HAVE OUTLIVED THEIR ENTHUSIASM AND LOST THEIR PERSPECTIVE.

Vitamins. Nutritional supplements. Mud packs. Face creams. Face lifts. Miracle diets. America abounds with weapons to fight old age. And with good reason—some people fear aging more than they fear monsters or even an IRS audit.

Yet age is not an enemy to you, the child of God. You are eternal. So view your time as a chance to grow closer to Him, to store up treasures in heaven, and to bring a bit of heaven to life on earth. And never forget that your ultimate destiny is with your Father—with an ageless body in a timeless paradise.

It's not how old you are, but how you are old.

MARIE DRESSLER

IF I REALLY WANTED TO
GROW CLOSER TO GOD,
I WOULD . . .

NEVER WRONGLY ACCUSE HIM

FINGERS POINTED IN ACCUSATION AT GOD WOULD BE BETTER OFF FOLDED IN PRAYER.

Because God is all-powerful, it's possible to assume He causes *everything* that happens. But that isn't the case. People are responsible for their own actions. And there are other forces at work, wreaking pain and deceit on the world. That is not God's way. There are things He won't do. He won't tempt you to break the rules of right living, and He won't kick you when you're down.

If you're at odds with God over a perceived misdeed, realize that He doesn't do anything to make His children bitter. So let go of the resentment you harbor and ask forgiveness for your lack of faith. Be at peace with your perfect Father.

How great is your goodness, which you have stored up for those who fear you, which you bestow in the sight of men on those who take refuge in you.

PSALM 31:19

IF I REALLY WANTED TO
GROW CLOSER TO GOD,
I WOULD . . .

LISTEN
TO
HIM

GOD HASN'T LOST HIS VOICE, BUT SOME PEOPLE HAVE LOST THE ABILITY TO LISTEN.

It's impossible to have a close relationship without communication. And listening is vital. We must listen to God. He may not speak with a thundering voice from the heavens anymore, but neither is He silent. His voice is no less clear than it ever was. You may hear it through a Scripture passage, a sermon, a song on the radio, even the words of a child.

However God's voice comes to you, God's Spirit in you and your knowledge of the Scriptures will help you know when God is speaking to you. And remember to go beyond hearing His words—respond to them as well.

My sheep listen to my voice; I know them, and they follow me.

JOHN 10:27

IF I REALLY WANTED TO
GROW CLOSER TO GOD,
I WOULD . . .

TURN AWAY FROM PREJUDICE

To God, there is only one race: the human race.

Jesus fervently prayed to God that believers "be brought to complete unity to let the world know that you sent me . . . " (John 17:23). Unfortunately, there are many things that hinder unity. Racism, for example, breeds hatred and misunderstanding and undermines the spiritual lives of believers.

Imagine what God thinks when some of His creation think they are better than others simply because of their skin color. Pray every day for racial harmony, and pursue relationships with people of different races. As you do this, you will help bring an answer to Jesus' prayer, and you can be sure that the heart of the God who plays no favorites will be with you.

We must learn to live together like brothers or we will perish together like fools.

Martin Luther King Jr.

Also Available in This Series:

If I Really Wanted to Simplify my Life, I Would . . .
If I Really Wanted to Be Happy, I Would . . .
If I Really Wanted to Lose Weight, I Would . . .
If I Really Wanted to Have a Great Marriage, I Would . . .
If I Really Wanted to Be a Great Friend, I Would . . .
If I Really Wanted to Make a Difference, I Would . . .
If I Really Wanted to Beat Stress, I Would . . .

If you have enjoyed this book, or if it has impacted your life, we would love to hear from you.

Please contact us at:

info@honorbooks.com